Stop Managing: Star

THE WORKBOOK F WINNING TEAMS

By Nathan Jamail

TO BE USED IN CONJUNCTION WITH ***THE SALES LEADERS PLAYBOOK***

Coach your employees to excellence!

Don't manage them to mediocrity!

Stop managing and start coaching!

Build a winning team!

Workbook Description

This workbook works in conjunction with *The Sales Leaders Playbook*. Reading the playbook and completing the exercises in this workbook will help you develop the skills you need to build a winning team. These exercises are not based on theory, but rather on proven techniques and practices that have allowed hundreds of sales teams to find success!

This workbook is intended for small workgroups or individual use. Leaders will learn the power of creating a winning culture and will therefore accomplish:

- Increased morale among team members and employees
- Improved skills and abilities
- Improved communication
- Increases in sales and profits

What you will need to complete this workbook:

- A copy of *The Sales Leaders Playbook*
- Pen or pencil
- Printed copy of this workbook
- An open and ready mind

Let's get started!

lead·er·ship n. 1. *an ability to lead*

Successful leadership does not come from simply observing and learning what a great leader says and does. In fact, most leaders *know* what it takes to be a great leader, but simply cannot find the time, or know how to prioritize their time, to make it a way of life. Successful leadership can only be acquired from *doing* it and doing it again and again. It is a habit. With practice, you can build and maintain the habit of successful leadership.

Make the Time

What did you do on your previous workday? Write down *exactly* what you did:

7:00am____

8:00am____

9:00am____

10:00am_______________________________________

11:00am_______________________________________

12:00pm_______________________________________

1:00pm____

2:00pm____

3:00pm____

4:00pm____

5:00pm____

6:00pm____

7:00pm____

Was this a productive day? Yes / No Why?____________________________

Did you accomplish at least three things that will help your employees grow and will therefore grow your business? Yes / No Circle those accomplishments.

"Know your goals. Pursue them as if you were chasing a player just ten yards away from a touchdown."

To succeed you must stay on target to achieve your leadership goals. The first step is to write down exactly what you want to accomplish. This is the hardest step!

Write down your top leadership goals. Not company goals or team goals, leadership goals.

For example:

"I would like to work at least three hours per week with Susie to help develop her talents."

Leadership Goal:____

Leadership Goal:____

Leadership Goal:____

Leadership Goal:____

Leadership Goal:____

"To cross the finish line, you must put your attributes into action."

Leaders have attributes and skills that contribute to their success. Attributes are inherent; we are often born with them. Many of us, for example, are born with the desire to succeed. While we are born with particular attributes, we can strengthen them and gain new ones by learning from valuable life lessons. Skills, on the other hand, are learned or taught. Language is an example of a skill. No one is born knowing a language. We learn a language because somebody teaches us.

What are the top attributes and skills that you *have*?

Attributes	Skills
1.________________	1.________________
2.________________	2.________________
3.________________	3.________________
4.________________	4.________________
5.________________	5.________________

What are the top attributes and skills that you *want*?

Attributes	Skills
1.________________	1.________________
2.________________	2.________________
3.________________	3.________________
4.________________	4.________________
5.________________	5.________________

"Making your weakest player a linebacker or your player with the poorest aim your quarterback will lead to unhappy players and many lost games."

A successful leader must be a *great coach*. A coach is a person that improves his team on a regular basis. No matter how good your team members are they can *always* improve and learn. A *great coach* will focus on the team's *strengths* and continue to push every individual to improve his or her greatest abilities in order to compensate for any weaknesses.

If you could line up your employees with a new fresh start, what position would they be in? Would you make your bottom sales person your administrative assistant? Your administrative assistant a sales person?

The Line Up

List your employees or team members below and what position each is currently in. Under the Line Up section, note whether each person is in the right position (same), a good employee but in the wrong position (change), or an employee who doesn't fit in the team or the company (not a fit). Feel free to use initials or code names for confidentiality reasons. In the Plan Section, explain the steps needed to help the employee move to a place where he or she fits.

Name　　　　Current Position　　　　Line Up

________________________　________________________　____________________________

Plan:____

Name　　　　Current Position　　　　Line Up

________________________　________________________　____________________________

Plan:____

Name　　　　Current Position　　　　Line Up

________________________　________________________　____________________________

Plan:____

Name Current Position Line Up

Plan:

Name Current Position Line Up

Plan:

Name Current Position Line Up

Plan:

Name Current Position Line Up

Plan:

Name Current Position Line Up

Plan:

Name Current Position Line Up

Plan:

Name Current Position Line Up

Plan:

Name Current Position Line Up

Plan:

"If you are not missing baskets, you are not taking enough shots."

Questions for Reflection

1. How does a football coach (or coach of any sport) improve the attributes and skills of his players? What lessons can you as a sales coach draw from his example?

   ____

   ____

   ____

2. Why should a coach place members of his team in positions where they fit best?

   ____

   ____

   ____

3. How can you encourage your team to come to you with more than just complaints?

   ____

   ____

   ____

4. What is a sign that you are not making enough decisions?

   ____

   ____

   ____

5. How is showing confidence related to displaying competence?

   ____

   ____

   ____

Sharing The Vision

THE SALES LEADERS PLAYBOOK

vi·sion n. 1. *an optimistic view of where the organization wants to be at a set time in the future*

When creating a vision, a leader must have an understanding of where his organization is and where he wants to go. The vision of the business gives it energy. It helps motivate employees in the direction of corporate strategy. It is the image that a business must have of its goals before it sets out to reach them. It describes aspirations for the future, without specifying the means that will be used to achieve those desired ends.

Examples of corporate vision statements:

GE – We bring good things to life.

Ford – To become the world's leading consumer company for automotive products and services.

Microsoft – To enable people and businesses throughout the world to realize their full potential.

What is your company vision statement?

____

What is your team vision statement?

____

To help develop your vision:

1. Brainstorm and write down all the things that might be possible for your organization to accomplish in a given time frame:

2. Edit the list to what you are willing to commit to:

Sharing The Vision

THE SALES LEADERS PLAYBOOK

"When you pass the vision to your team members, they must have the understanding and skills to carry it successfully across the field and to the goal."

Refer to your organization's vision statement when answering the following questions.

1. How will your vision benefit the organization as a whole? (Give at least three benefits).

   ____

   ____

   ____

2. How will the achievement of the vision benefit each team member? (Be specific).

   ____

   ____

   ____

3. What are your expectations for your team?

   ____

   ____

   ____

4. What is your plan of action and business plan for achieving your vision?

   ____

   ____

   ____

5. How do you know that your team members understand the vision?

   ____

   ____

   ____

On a separate sheet of paper, construct an outline of how you will present the vision to your team.

cul·ture n. 1. *The sum total of ways of living built up by a group of human beings transmitted from one generation to another.*

Creating a winning culture is probably the single most important aspect of success. In societies around the world, people's beliefs, ideas, laws and rules for conduct are formed and developed by the culture in which they live. The culture of a society is one of the most powerful influences on a person.

Positioning people – Organizing a Winning Culture

As stated in Successful Leadership, having the right people in the right place is critical. There are three important aspects to look at when positioning people effectively:

- A person's interests or likes
- A person's attributes
- A person's skill set

Take the time to list what skills and attributes are needed for each ***position*** you lead. Use an additional sheet of paper for more positions.

Position	Skills Needed	Attributes Needed
____________	________________________	________________________
	________________________	________________________
	________________________	________________________

Position	Skills Needed	Attributes Needed
____________	________________________	________________________
	________________________	________________________
	________________________	________________________

"Every day is a draft day!"

Tough Decision Making

There comes a point in the process of creating a winning culture when you realize someone may not fit anywhere. This is the time to make the decision that someone may fit better in a different position or in a different company.

Set your team standards. Below is a starting point; add your own.

1. A winning attitude-*always.*
2. Each team member has the right attributes.
3. Each team member is a top performer.
4. Each team member must practice.
5. ____
6. ____
7. ____
8. ____

Team Accountability

List the names of your top performers (those with whom you should spend most of your coaching time) and opportunities you have to work with them:

____

____

____

____

____

____

____

"A winning environment is a like strong wind at your back: it pushes you and your team forward to your goal."

The advantage of team *buy-in* comes when the leader is no longer the only one holding the team members accountable. Achieving team *buy-in* requires the following steps: sharing with your team your plan for creating a winning environment, showing them the results and rewards of the environment, and obtaining the team's commitment.

As a team leader, how would you handle the following situations?

1. Everyone on your sales team has bought into creating a winning culture by holding one another accountable—except one member of the team. This member of the team, however, is consistently your top performer.

   ____
   ____
   ____
   ____
   ____
   ____

2. One of your bottom performers complains to you repeatedly that you play favorites because you spend most of your coaching time with the top performers.

   ____
   ____
   ____
   ____
   ____
   ____

trans·form v. 1. *To change the form of; to change in appearance.*

Belief systems provide a core set of values on which we base everything we do, say or believe. A business's belief system set the precepts from which it conducts business, those that govern its planning, direction, and actions.

Before you can transform a belief system, you have to identify the current belief system. What is the current belief system of your business?

____

____

It's not just what you know, it's what you do.

Now that you know the current belief system, let's change it or line it up!

If your business is truly based on a belief system, then you should be able to provide evidence of this belief system in the practices of your business. If you cannot provide evidence, then perhaps it's time to change your belief system or line up your business practices with the belief system you are supposed to have.

What evidence supports the belief system you identified above?

____

____

____

Does your belief system lead to success? Why or why not?

____

____

____

Do you think your belief system needs to be transformed? If so, how will you change it?

____

____

____

"You can't steal second base while keeping a foot on first."

Questions for Reflection

1. How is the belief system the nucleus of the organization?

2. Why would it be advantageous for an organization to change its belief system over time?

3. How does a company's belief system affect its performance?

4. What can happen if not everyone on a team really believes the belief system?

5. How does a successful leader uphold a belief system in stormy waters?

prac·tice v. 1. *To exercise one's self in, for improvement, or to acquire discipline or dexterity*

In sales we spend less than 1% of the time practicing and 99% of the time playing the game. Why are we overlooking the most important element of the game?

Weekly Team Practices

Weekly team practices should not go over an hour and a half. A sample agenda:

8:00am	Weekly sales recognition
8:10am	Skill training
8:50am	Company and team updates
9:05am	Roundtable discussion
9:15am	Meeting adjourned

Skill training should be applicable to your business and tailored appropriately. These should not be *product* training meetings, but ***skill*** trainings – skills such as tele-prospecting, closing, etc. ONE skill should be practiced for two weeks before moving on to another skill.

Develop a team-wide practice plan focusing on negotiation skills, training skills, selling skills, and role-playing. Explain how you will incorporate this plan into your weekly meetings.

____

____

____

____

____

____

Below is a sample agenda that you can fill in and use for your trainings. Brackets are for start times to help keep you on track.

Sales Practice Training

Date____________________ Time____________________

- (   ) Sales Recognition:____

  ____

- (   ) Skill Training:____

  ____

  ____

  ____

  ____

  ____

- (   ) Company/Team Updates:____

  ____

  ____

  ____

  ____

  ____

- (   ) Roundtable Discussion
- (   ) Meeting Adjourned; now go practice what you learned!
- Notes

  ____

  ____

  ____

  ____

  ____

  ____

  ____

  ____

  ____

  ____

Practice Makes Profit

THE SALES LEADERS PLAYBOOK

"A salesperson who doesn't practice is like a marathon runner who never trains her mind, lungs, will, and muscles."

Monthly Group Practices

Each month, coordinate groups within the organization to get together and practice. Select from the sample list of skills below or choose your own. This group practice should last approximately two to three hours.

Quarterly Division Practices

Once per quarter, all individuals within a division should spend an entire day practicing skills. This is also a good time for recognition and rewards. This division practice should last approximately 6-8 hours. *Sample list of skills to focus on (input additional skills applicable for your business on the blank lines):*

- In-Person prospecting
- Tele-prospecting
- Cold calling
- Working current database or sphere (past or present clients)
- Presentation skills
- Negotiation
- Building rapport
- Understanding customer needs
- Mapping customer solutions
- Overcoming objections
- Closing
- ______________________________
- ______________________________
- ______________________________

You can also offer leadership skills training:

- *Handling HR issues*
- *Coaching*
- *Motivating*
- *Giving feedback*
- *Addressing conflict*
- *Planning*
- *Budgeting*
- *Building team empowerment*

"Practice prepares the salesperson to move gracefully with the unexpected, like an proficient surfer perfectly balanced between wind and wave."

Role-Playing

Role-playing gives you a sense of each of your team member's attributes, skills, strengths, and weaknesses. Role-playing gives them much needed practice and concrete lessons.

Listed below are situations for you to role-play with your team. You may also create your own. For each one, note how your salesperson played out the scenario, what skills and attributes were put into practice, your thoughts on the performance, and how you will coach this salesperson based on the role-play.

An angry former customer confronts your salesperson in view of several potential buyers, falsely claiming that the salesperson tricked him into buying a faulty product.

Actions of your salesperson: ______________________________

____

____

Attributes and skills put into practice: ______________________________

Thoughts on performance: ______________________________

How you will coach: ______________________________

A customer expresses interest in the product your salesperson is selling. She knows a lot about the product of the competition, which your salesperson knows is superior, but not much about your product.

Actions of your salesperson: ______________________________

____

____

Attributes and skills put into practice: ______________________________

Thoughts on performance: ______________________________

How you will coach: ______________________________

Scenario: ____

____

____

Actions of your salesperson: ______________________________

____

____

Attributes and skills put into practice: ______________________

Thoughts on performance: ________________________________

How you will coach: ____________________________________

Scenario: ____

____

____

Actions of your salesperson: ______________________________

____

____

Attributes and skills put into practice: ______________________

Thoughts on performance: ________________________________

How you will coach: ____________________________________

Scenario: ____

____

____

Actions of your salesperson: ______________________________

____

____

Attributes and skills put into practice: ______________________

Thoughts on performance: ________________________________

How you will coach: ____________________________________

Practice Makes Profit

"A winning team needs a coach who practices coaching."

Understanding the Need for Practice

1. Explain how salesmanship is an art form comprised of intangibles such as attitudes, egos, emotions, and energy.

2. How does practice prepare your team for such intangibles?

ex·pec·ta·tion n. 1. *That which is expected or looked for.*

One of the major causes of problems which managers face today is unclear expectations between them and their team. Successful managers make expectations very clear so that their team can respond and acknowledge they understand and accept what their manager wants from them.

What is the "Surprise Theory"?

____

____

Setting Expectations for Your Team: List expectations according to the requirements on page 73 of the Sales Leaders Playbook. Continue on an additional sheet if needed.

1) ____
2) ____
3) ____
4) ____
5) ____
6) ____
7) ____
8) ____
9) ____
10) ____
11) ____
12) ____
13) ____
14) ____
15) ____

Setting Clear Expectations

THE SALES LEADERS PLAYBOOK

"Failure to communicate your expectations is akin to coaching with meaningless expressions and gestures."

Why is it important for leaders to prioritize their expectations?

____

____

What is the difference between an activity and a task?

____

Expectations for Yourself: Input items your team can expect from you; see sample on page 74 and 75 of the Sales Leaders Playbook. Use an additional sheet if needed.

1) ____
2) ____
3) ____
4) ____
5) ____
6) ____
7) ____
8) ____
9) ____
10) ____
11) ____
12) ____
13) ____
14) ____
15) ____

ac·count·able n. 1. *Capable of being accounted for; explicable.*

At the organizational (or team) level, accountability is the acknowledgement of responsibility for actions, decisions, and policies, and the obligation to report, explain and be answerable for the resulting consequences. It means *no excuses*. The willingness to be accountable for what you do and what you fail or refuse to do is crucial to success.

Why should you hold your team accountable?

____

____

What are the consequences for not meeting the expectations outlined earlier?

____

____

____

____

Does your team know these consequences? YES NO

No, my team doesn't, but they will by this date: ________________________

What style is best for confronting an employee who is not meeting expectations?

____

____

How will you hold yourself accountable before your team?

____

____

Holding Your Team Accountable

THE SALES LEADERS PLAYBOOK

"The swordfighter who evades responsibility and parries accountability will, more often than not, feel the sting of a hit."

Do members of your team constantly make excuses? YES NO

What excuses do you hear the most?

____

____

____

____

How do you respond to these excuses?

____

____

____

____

Do your responses hold your team members accountable?

____

____

If not, how will you hold them accountable in the future?

____

____

____

____

Developing a Business Plan

plan n. 1. *A way of procedure; a method of action*

Many companies talk about having plans and the importance of them; however, few actually utilize them fully. It is not uncommon for individuals and organizations to struggle with creating a business plan, but the purpose of a business plan is to turn thoughts and ideas into intentional behaviors and actions. A business plan is therefore critical to business operations.

Everyone develops a business plan. Now develop yours!

Grab a separate paper or use the format at the end of this section and sketch out your business plan. Later, transfer to a document to share with your team and a template to give to each team member to fill out. Keep in mind a business plan should be S.M.A.R.T.

S – Specific (as detailed as possible)

M – Measurable (goals can be measured)

A – Achievable (goals are realistic, but still a reach)

R – Relevant (applicable to the job required and to the marketplace)

T – Timetabled (set dates and time frames to achieve goals)

Business Plan Outline

- Time frame of business plan (typically quarterly)
- Include expectations that you outlined earlier
    - For each expectation list at least two action items to exceed the expectation that follow the S.M.A.R.T. objectives.
    - Include measures and time frames of achievement for each expectation.

Developing a Business Plan

THE SALES LEADERS PLAYBOOK

"Does a football team take the field without a game plan?"

Presenting plans as a team is critical in creating ownership of the plan and should be done on a quarterly basis. Each presenter should have at least 30 minutes to present his plan and answer questions. You and your team should be a presentation schedule. Below are some guidelines.

Presentation Review

- Introduction review
    - Who you are?
    - What team you represent?
- Outlook of your team or division
- List all major goals with at least two ways you will exceed each one
- List accomplishments in last quarter and/or how you met the last goals you presented (accountability)
- List best practices to share with the team
- List obstacles to gain ideas and discussion from the team, but do not let this become a gripe session
- Wrap up with Q & A

Sample Timeframe for Presentations

Quarterly Presentation Schedule	*1st Qtr*	*2nd Qtr*	*3rd Qtr*	*4th Qtr*
• VP Level Review	Dec 28	Feb 28	May 28	Aug 28
• Director Level Review	Jan 15	March 15	June 15	Sept 15
• Manager Level Review	Jan 30	March 30	June 30	Sept 30

Schedule your next (or 1st) presentation: ______________________________

Schedule your team presentation: ______________________________

Developing a Business Plan

"Not having goals in your business plan is like not including the hoop in your basketball game strategy."

As a leader, your job is not only to have your plan and to ensure your team has a plan, but also to enforce, assist and develop plans with your team.

What is YOUR goal for your team members?

Name______________________________Goal__________________________

____

How can YOU help them?____

Name______________________________Goal__________________________

____

How can YOU help them?____

Name______________________________Goal__________________________

____

How can YOU help them?____

Name______________________________Goal__________________________

____

How can YOU help them____

Name______________________________Goal__________________________

____

How can YOU help them?____

On the following pages is a sample simple business plan to get you and your team started.

Business Plan

Timeframe: Name:

Company Vision/Mission Statement:

Last Quarter's Results:

This Quarter's Goals:

Specific Goal # 1:

How to achieve it:

1.

2.

Date to accomplished:

Specific Goal # 2:

How to achieve it:

1.

2.

Date to accomplished:

Specific Goal # 3:

How to achieve it:

1.

2.

Date to accomplished:

Specific Goal # 4:

How to achieve it:

1.

2.

Date to accomplished:

Specific Goal # 5:

How to achieve it:

1.

2.

Date to accomplished:

Additional Notes/Expectations:

Did you meet the goals from the last plan? If not, what can you do differently?

Questions for Review

1. Why do business plans get delayed?

2. Why should business plans be constantly adjusted?

3. Why do employees need to take ownership of the business plan?

4. How do business plans help us keep our eye on the prize?

coach·ing v. 1. *To impart, as knowledge before unknown, or rules for practice; to train by special instructions; to direct.*

One-on-one coaching sessions are key to successful leadership. These sessions go well beyond giving straightforward instruction. They involve more than just sitting down with an employee for 30-45 minutes shooting the breeze or giving updates. It is a structured coaching activity intended to deliver clear insights and specific results.

Step one: Schedule a session with each team member and inform each member of what you plan to cover in that one-on-one coaching session.

Pick a date and write it down. This scheduled event is MORE IMPORTANT than meeting with a customer. Make the time!

Team member name: ______________________ Date of One-on-One: __________________
Team member name: ______________________ Date of One-on-One: __________________
Team member name: ______________________ Date of One-on-One: __________________
Team member name: ______________________ Date of One-on-One: __________________
Team member name: ______________________ Date of One-on-One: __________________
Team member name: ______________________ Date of One-on-One: __________________
Team member name: ______________________ Date of One-on-One: __________________

Step two: Develop an agenda.

- Always conduct them in an office without distractions
- Be consistent
- Have an agenda
- Stay on point
- Make it a priority
- Keep it to a maximum of one hour
- Keep it from becoming a gripe meeting

Use the following sample agenda outline for your next one-on-one; keep them and reference them for each one-on-one coaching session.

Team Member One-On-One

Team Member Name: ______________________________ Date: ____________

1. Review weekly pipeline, pending sales and last week's results:
   - Pipeline______________________________
   - Pending sales______________________________
   - Last week's results______________________________
2. Go over previous and current week's scheduled appointments:
   - Previous weeks appointments______________________________
   - Scheduled appointments______________________________
3. Set three activity goals for the week and review the previous week's goals:
   - Previous week's goals and achievements

     1: ______________________________

     2: ______________________________

     3: ______________________________
   - This week's goals

     1: ______________________________

     2: ______________________________

     3: ______________________________

4. Discuss any major prospects or customers and identify an action plan with them:
   - Prospect/Customer: ____

     ____
   - Prospect/Customer: ____

     ____
   - Prospect/Customer: ____

     ____
5. Work on sales skills development:
   - Skill: ____
6. Role-play a sales call or prospecting call to practice:
   - Scenario: ____

Additional Items for Sales Managers

- Discuss each person on their respective team:
  - Team member____

    ____
  - Team member____

    ____
  - Team member____

    ____
  - Team member____

    ____
  - Team member____

    ____
- Review any possible new candidates and check status of the bench of prospective sales reps:
  - ____
  - ____
- Review business plan and activity status:
  - ____
- Develop next week's training topic for their next team practice.

Effective Sales Meetings

ef·fec·tive adj. 1. *Producing a decided, decisive, or desired result; impressive, striking.*

Have you ever said or thought, "Sales meetings are a waster of time"? If you, your team, or organization wonders why you have sales meetings, then it is time for a change. To begin, stop having sales meetings to review what is happening, what is not happening, and giving out new company information. Instead, start conducting weekly sales *practices*. This was also briefly covered in "Practice Makes Profits".

Weekly sales practices have three components:

1. Recognition - Recognize the team; put a recognition program in place if you do not have one and be sure to show your appreciation for the team's efforts.

   What is your recognition program:

   ____

2. Communication - Review what is necessary with your team and then move on; do not let your practice sessions turn into complaint sessions.

3. Practice - Pick a skill to work on for two weeks at a time so that you will cover 25 skills in a year (assuming two weeks off for holiday). Repeat skills if necessary.

   Write down the skills that will cover the next six months:

   1. ____________________ ____________________
   2. ____________________ ____________________
   3. ____________________ ____________________
   4. ____________________ ____________________
   5. ____________________ ____________________
   6. ____________________ ____________________

Sample Meeting Agenda - Use this as a guide to form your own practice sessions:

"Qualifying" Team Practice Schedule	
8:00 am	Recognition Program
8:10 am	Qualifying Training
	(How to effectively qualify prospective customers)
8:50 am	Company and Team Updates
9:05 am	Round Table Discussions
9:15 am	Meeting Adjourned

Now put together your next agenda in order to keep you on task:

"________________________________" ***Team Practice Schedule***

Date: ____________________

Time	Topic
__________	______________________________________
__________	______________________________________
__________	______________________________________
__________	______________________________________
__________	______________________________________
__________	______________________________________
__________	______________________________________

Effective Sales Meetings

THE SALES LEADERS PLAYBOOK

"Effective sales meetings will make your sales team a championship team."

Be as specific and concrete as possible in answering the following questions. Moreover, don't just write the answers in this workbook; incorporate the answers into your sales meetings!

1. How will you transform your sales meetings into practice meetings?

____

____

____

____

2. How will you make these meetings motivational and energetic?

____

____

____

____

3. How will you give your team members the recognition they desire?

____

____

____

____

4. How will you encourage *healthy* internal competition?

____

____

____

____

pro·duc·tive adj. 1. *Yielding results, benefits, or profit; the power to produce, especially in abundance.*

As a leader, it is imperative for you to know what is going on in the field with your team and customers. In the past, many managers found themselves managing from the "ivory tower." Today, managers are striving to get in the field and take a more "hands on" approach. Yet they find themselves more than ever tied to the office in management meetings, dealing with HR issues, and bound to their email and PDA device. There are ways to ensure that leaders focus and stay in the streets with their team. The first step is to commit to the idea of it.

Think of your priorities, not your expectations, but your priorities. What are they?

1. ______________________________

2. ______________________________

3. ______________________________

4. ______________________________

5 . ______________________________

If your priorities do not put you with your team in the field more than 50% of the time, then you may want to revisit your priorities. Being in the streets with your team allows you to *show* them, *coach* them, and *develop* them. In short, to be a leader.

Productive Street Days

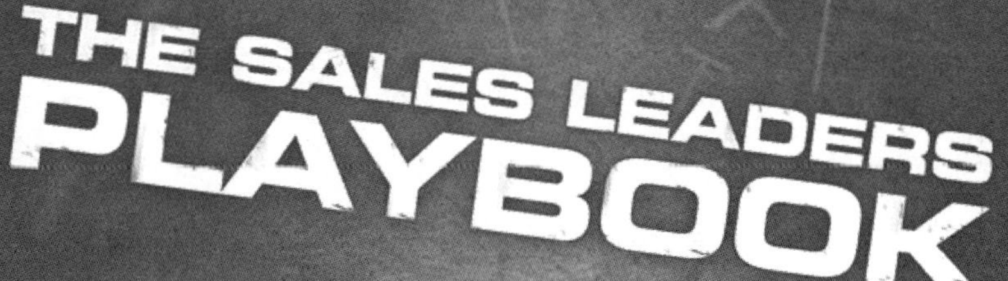

List ways that you can coach while on the street:

Example: Following a sales call, role-play how things could have gone differently.

1. ______________________________

2. ______________________________

3. ______________________________

Take the time right now to schedule a street day for you and each of your team members:

Team Member: ____________________ Next Street Day: ______________

Team Member: ____________________ Next Street Day: ______________

Team Member: ____________________ Next Street Day: ______________

Team Member: ____________________ Next Street Day: ______________

Team Member: ____________________ Next Street Day: ______________

By now, you are trying to figure out ways to schedule everything you have learned. Following are some sample calendars and outlines.

Sample Daily, Weekly, Monthly, Quarterly Schedules

(Adjust times, days, etc. to fit your business model)

Daily/Weekly

- 7:30 am — Arrive at the office; greet everyone and spread positive energy
- 8:00 am — Team practice (once per week; other days fill in with one-on-ones)
- 9:30 am — Administrative
- 11:30 am — One-on-one with a team member (if one-on-one sessions are complete, fill in with follow-up, administrative)
- 12:30 pm — Lunch with a client or prospect
- 2:00 pm — Street time with a team member
- 4:30 pm — Back to office; administrative
- 5:30 pm — Conclude day

Monthly/Quarterly

1st Quarter: Month one, week one

- Prepare your business plan and expectations for your team

1st Quarter: Month one, week two

- Deliver expectations and your business plan to team members during your one-on-one meetings and request theirs to be ready to present by a specific date as outlined below

1st Quarter: Month one, week four

- Each team member to present business plans to the entire team
- Advise your team of the upcoming quarterly practice for all team members, plan out curriculum and topic

1st Quarter: Month two, week two

- 6-8 hour all hands team practice

Repeat each quarter.

Taking the Bullet

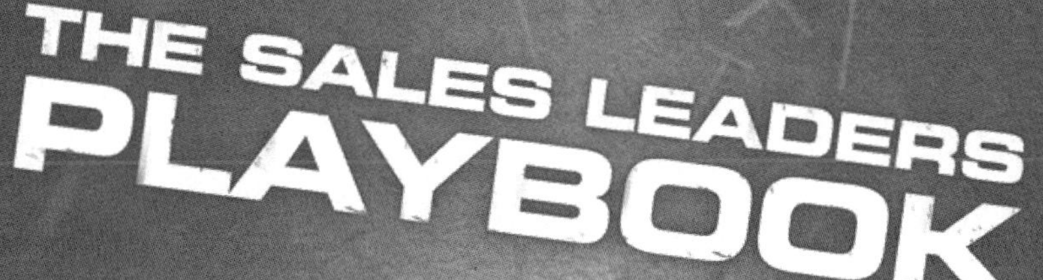

bul·let n. 1. *A round missile to be fired with a firearm; a very fast and accurately thrown ball.*

Explain what you, as a sales leader, would do in the following situations:

1. You find that your leadership style is very effective at achieving successful sales, but is not very well liked by half of your team.

____

____

____

____

____

____

2. You know exactly what you and your team need to do to succeed, but while your plan is perfectly ethical, it goes against the wishes of someone higher up the chain of command.

____

____

____

____

____

____

3. You have an outstanding sales team, but you sense from them uncertainty that you would take a bullet for them.

____

____

____

____

____

____

Review THE SALES LEADERS PLAYBOOK

Circle TRUE (T) or FALSE (F) for each of the following statements.

T / F 1. Successful leadership is both an attribute and a skill.

T / F 2. It is solely your team's responsibility to make sure they understand the vision.

T / F 3. Positioning people where they best fit doesn't allow them to grow.

T / F 4. Transforming a belief system means compromising one's principles.

T / F 5. Every sales team should strive to be Number One.

T / F 6. Salesmanship is one of the hardest skills in any profession.

T / F 7. Any great salesperson can be a great sales coach.

T / F 8. Successful managers make expectations very clear.

T / F 9. A winning team strives to exceed expectations.

T / F 10. A good sales coach recognizes first downs, not just touchdowns.

T / F 11. Trusting means not having to verify.

T / F 12. The purpose of a business plan is to turn thoughts into actions.

T / F 13. Your team should be involved in drafting the business plan.

T / F 14. Talking to your employees daily adequately substitutes for one-on-ones.

T / F 15. You should turn your sales meetings into practice meetings.

T / F 16. Street days are perfect for coaching.

T / F 17. A good sales coach knows and appreciates what motives each member of the team.

T / F 18. Being a great leader means not being afraid to get fired.

See answers on page 44.

Review

THE SALES LEADERS PLAYBOOK

In the next few weeks, how are you going to implement the principles, programs and strategies of *The Sales Leaders Playbook*? Be specific.

NOW GO DO IT!

Final Thoughts

I hope you have enjoyed *The Sales Leaders Playbook* and this workbook and that they have brought value to you and your team. I am not a writer by trade; I am a sales person who has successfully led sales teams across the country. I hope you decide to implement programs in this workbook and even from other great books to help you become an even greater coach.

The topics covered are not rocket science, but they do take time and commitment to implement. When implemented on a consistent basis, they enable any sales team to become a number one top performing sales team. I look forward to hearing about your future success!

-Nathan Jamail

Answers for review on page 42.

1. T	10. T
2. F	11. F
3. F	12. T
4. F	13. T
5. T	14. F
6. T	15. T
7. F	16. T
8. T	17. T
9. T	18. T